Presented to

Claire Walsh

from

Church of the Nativity

on

February 12, 2002

THE BIBLE

THE BIBLE

AS NARRATED BY JESUS, THE STORYTELLER

Text
Louis M. Savary
William E. Frankhauser

Creative Concept and Layout
Edward Letwenko

Cover and Text Illustrations
Edward Letwenko

THE REGINA PRESS
New York

THE REGINA PRESS
145 Sherwood Avenue
Farmingdale, New York

ISBN: 0-88271-198-9

PRINTED IN BELGIUM

*This book is dedicated to the memory of
Edmond C. Malhame,
whose love, courage and determination
were a great inspiration to all of us
at The Regina Press.*

Contents

A Word for Teachers and Parents

The Bible is different. As the Storyteller presents bible stories to his class, the children become totally involved. They feel free to ask whatever questions occur to them and to share personal reactions with one another. By so involving themselves, the children learn to see the world from God's viewpoint, and they begin to understand how their very own lives become a part of the continuing story of God's people.

The stories selected portray major biblical events. Remaining faithful to the traditional text, each story expresses in simple language a theological message that is supportive, hopeful and loving.

The text is enhanced by more than fifty illustrations of great charm and appeal. The past and present, the unknown and the familiar, all are blended together with imagination and charm. In this way, biblical events many centuries old are brought into the immediate focus of a child's world.

The Bible may be used as a text for teaching bible class to younger children or as a collection of biblical stories for children of any age.

Reading about the Storyteller and his young friends may also prove just as revealing to grownups as to children. In fact, many adults who read this book in manuscript said they wished they had been told bible stories in this informal, childlike way. For as Jesus said, "Unless you become like children, you will not be able to find your way into God's kingdom."

The Bible

As Narrated By Jesus, The Storyteller

Sunday School Class

"I wonder why our Sunday School teacher isn't here yet," said Linda.

"Don't worry," said Gail. "She'll be here soon."

"But it's late," said Linda. "I hope she's okay."

"I've got an idea," said Gail. "Let's hide under the table and surprise her."

"Okay," agreed Linda.

Sitting together beneath the table, they looked at each other and giggled.

Around the room, other children were making noise and having fun. One boy, sitting in the teacher's chair, rested his new shoes on her big desk.

Another boy at his own desk was busy drawing a picture of Gail and Linda in red and yellow crayon.

Tom and Jennifer were playing tic-tac-toe at the chalkboard.

Just then a new boy stood in the doorway.

From under the table, Gail and Linda noticed him. Linda whispered to Gail, "I wonder who he is."

"I never saw him before," answered Gail.
He's bigger than we are," said Linda.
"But not too much bigger," replied Gail.
"He's older than we are," whispered Linda.
"But not too much older," answered Gail.
By this time, the other children had noticed the new boy and were looking at him.

"Hi, everybody," the boy in the doorway said. "I've come to stay with you until your teacher gets here."

"Who are you?" asked Gail, getting out from under the table.

"I'm a friend of your teacher's," said the new boy. "Would you like to hear some Bible stories while

we wait together?" He smiled and added, "They're fun."

"Okay," the children answered.

"Should we sit on our chairs?" asked Linda, who liked to know what she was supposed to do.

"Let's sit in a circle," suggested Bill, the boy who had been at the teacher's desk.

"Yes! I like circles," added Gail, moving her chair. The other children liked sitting in circles too.

Linda pulled her chair next to Gail's.

"I'm going to sit on the floor," said Bill.

"I'll sit next to you," laughed Jennifer. And she did.

So the class gathered around the new boy. Some sat on chairs, others sat on the floor.

"Has anyone here ever read the Bible?" the storyteller asked.

Some shook their heads no.

Jennifer answered, "It's too hard to read."

"And it's too long," said Gail sadly.

"It has too many big words," added Linda.

"We're too little to read the Bible by ourselves," said Tom.

The storyteller smiled at them. He knew how hard reading could be. Then he asked, "Would you like to know what's in the Bible?"

They all nodded yes together.

"Then let's begin," said the storyteller.

THE OLD
TESTAMENT

The Old Testament

(GENESIS 6:18 and 9:8–17)

ooking at the children gathered around him, the storyteller asked, "Do any of you have Bibles at home?"

"Sure," said Gail. "My mother and father have a big white Bible. We keep it on the coffee table in the living room."

"Our family Bible is very old," said Jennifer. "It belonged to my great-great-grandmother. Inside she wrote the names of all the people in her family."

"Our Bible has our names in it, too," said Gail.

"Our Bible has pictures of Bible people in it," added Bill. "I wonder what people were like then —I mean, when they wrote the Bible."

The other children wondered about biblical people too.

"I'll bet they were a lot like us," said Tom.

"That's right, Tom, the Bible is about people just like us," the storyteller explained, "except that the people in the Bible lived a long time ago. They were very special to God."

"Are we special to God?" asked Gail.

"Just like the people in the Bible?" added Linda.

"Yes, you are," answered the storyteller. "God says over and over that people are special to Him and that He loves them very much."

"How did people ever find out that God loved them?" asked Jennifer.

"And how did they find out they were special?" called out David.

"That's what the Bible stories are all about," answered the storyteller. "Each story explains God's love and care for us in a different way."

"I want to count all the different ways," said Gail, holding up her ten fingers.

"Maybe you'll need my fingers, too," added Linda, holding up her fingers.

"Don't forget our fingers," chimed in the boys.

They all laughed and held up their fingers, even the storyteller.

"The earliest stories of God's love came from the first part of the Bible," said the storyteller. "Does anyone know what names we call the two parts of the Bible?"

"Old and New," offered Bill. "Old and New something. I heard my father say the other word, but I can't remember it."

"Testament," added Jennifer, quite sure she was correct.

Bill turned to Jennifer and said, "That's right. That's the word my father used. The Old Testament and the New Testament."

"What's a Testament?" asked Gail.

"It's an agreement," explained the storyteller.

"The Old Testament tells about the first agreement between God and people."

"How did people know God was making an agreement with them?" asked Bill.

The storyteller answered, "One way God used was the rainbow. God said that whenever people saw a rainbow, they could be sure God was keeping His side of the agreement."

"I'm going to look for rainbows from now on," said Gail excitedly.

"Me, too," said Linda.

"The rainbow was one sign of the first agreement, the Old Testament," said the storyteller. "The people agreed to love, honor, and obey God, and God promised to love, cherish, and protect the people."

"Did the people do all those things they said they would?" asked Tom.

"Some of them did, and some of them didn't," answered the storyteller. "No matter what people did, though, God kept His side of the agreement, right from the beginning."

"Then let's start at the beginning," said Jennifer with a smile.

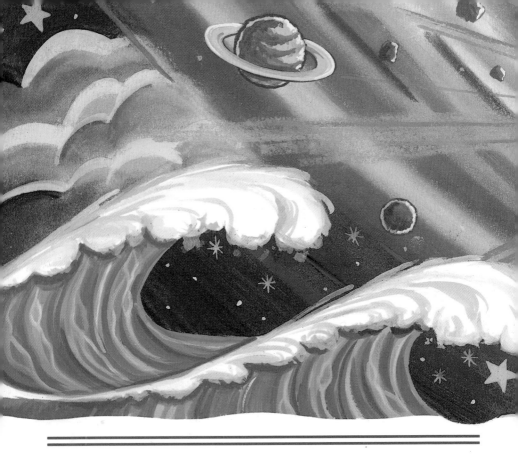

God Made the World

(GENESIS 1:1–2:3)

 n the beginning," said the new boy, "there was only God. There was no water, no earth, no sun, no moon; there were no stars, no trees, nor birds, nor songs. There were no days and nights. There were no angels—and no people."

Moving closer to Gail, Linda whispered, "It

must have been dark and lonely then."

"Empty, too, I'll bet," Tom added.

Bill suggested, "It must have been like when you close your eyes and can't see anything."

"Yes," answered the young storyteller. "That's the way it was in the beginning. But God's love would change all that. God made the oceans, the earth and the sky. He also made the sun for daytime and the moon for night. And He even put stars in the sky."

Then the storyteller asked, "Did anyone here ever plant a seed and watch it grow?"

"Yes," answered Jennifer, Bill, and Tom together.

"I did, too," Linda whispered to Gail.

"Well, that's what God did next," said the story-teller. "He created trees and flowers on the land, and these were able to produce seeds to grow other trees and flowers.

"But God wanted to share His love in another way. So He filled the land with animals and the oceans with fish and the sky with birds.

"Last of all, God saw a fuller way to share His love, and He made people."

"Like us?" asked Bill.

"Yes, just like all of us," answered the storyteller. "We are just like God because we can think and love. That's what God does all the time."

"God made people like us to be just like Him," said Gail with a smile.

"I think that was very nice of Him," added Linda.

"It took God six days to make the whole world," the storyteller went on. "And then—guess what He did on the seventh day."

"He took a rest period!" called out Jennifer. The class giggled and laughed. Jennifer often made the class laugh.

"Jennifer's right," said the storyteller, smiling. "On the seventh day God rested. God wanted to enjoy His world."

"The world needs time to rest, too," added Bill.

"Sunday is a day of rest," Jennifer said.

"Don't forget, Sunday is also God's day," said Gail, "a special day for being with God."

The storyteller agreed. "It's important for each of us to take the time we need—on any day—to be in touch with God.

Adam and Eve

(GENESIS 2:4–3:24)

 e like your stories," said Linda. "Please tell us another one."

"Yes! Tell us another story!" everyone cried.

So the young boy began again. "God called the first man He made Adam. He gave Adam a very beautiful place to live in. It was called Eden. All around Eden were plants and trees and beautiful flowers."

The storyteller asked the children to close their eyes and imagine the most beautiful garden they had ever seen.

"Eden was probably just like the pictures you have in your mind," he said.

"Then God saw another way to make Adam happier," he went on. "If Adam had somebody to love and to share his thoughts with, Adam would be more like God, who shared His love and thoughts with Adam. So God made Eve."

"Adam and Eve could do anything or go anywhere they wanted and eat whatever grew in the garden, except the fruit from one special tree. By asking them not to eat what grew on that one tree,

God was testing Adam and Eve, in a way. They were free to accept or refuse His love.

"One day Eve met a snake. This was a special snake, because before God had made Adam and Eve, He made angels. One angel refused God's love. This angel came to Eve as a snake and told Eve and Adam to go ahead and eat the fruit hanging from that tree. 'You'll become just like God if you do,' the snake said. And do you know what happened?"

"I'll bet they ate the fruit," called out Tom.

"Yes, they ate the fruit," said the storyteller. "And for the first time they had sad feelings that they never had before. They didn't know how to talk to God about what they had done, so they didn't say a word to God about it. But God knew."

"Does that mean Adam and Eve disobeyed God?" asked Linda.

"Yes," the storyteller answered. "And because they disobeyed God, they couldn't walk in the garden with Him anymore. Adam and Eve had refused God's love the way the angel had done. Now they had to leave their beautiful garden. But God promised Adam that He would find a way to make things right again between them and Himself. As they walked out of Eden, Adam and Eve felt very sad. For the first time in their lives, they knew what it was like to be without God."

"I'm sorry they listened to that bad snake," said Jennifer, shaking her head.

"I wouldn't like it if I had to leave God and try to do things without Him," said Bill.

Noah's Ark

(GENESIS 6:1–8:20)

 long, long time went by, hundreds of years, in fact, and pretty soon the earth was full of people. But these people found it hard to be good by themselves, because they didn't take the time to know and love God. Except Noah. He was a good man. God chose Noah and his family to give the world a chance to begin again, a new chance to know Him and love Him. So God told Noah to build an Ark."

"What's an Ark?" interrupted Tom.

"An Ark is a big boat," answered Bill. "My father told me that."

"God told Noah to take a pair of each kind of animal that He made," continued the storyteller. "So Noah and his family, and a pair of every kind of animal, went on board the Ark."

"Dogs and cats?" asked Gail.

"Horses and chickens?" asked Bill.

"Canaries and parakeets?" asked Linda.

"Every single kind of animal?" wondered David.

"Yes, said the storyteller. "Noah took on the Ark a mother and father for every single kind of animal. Then it rained. It rained for forty days, night and day, every day. When the rain stopped, the sky was blue again.

"There was a big rainbow in the sky. It was a sign from God that things were all right again.

The rainbow was God's promise that He would never again destroy the whole earth by a flood. Noah's Ark was the only thing floating under the big rainbow. Nothing else was saved—except the fish, who didn't even notice the rain. Noah and his family were the only people left to walk the earth.

"One day, after the rain stopped, Noah let a dove fly away from the Ark. When the dove didn't come back, Noah knew the bird had found dry land.

"The next morning, the boat stopped moving. Noah looked over the side of the boat. 'We're on dry land,' he shouted happily to everyone. 'All the water has disappeared.' "

"Where did it go?" asked Bill, who was full of questions.

"It's just like when water runs out of a tub," explained Jennifer. "It went down the drain!" Everyone laughed.

"So Noah and the others got off the Ark to live on the earth again," said the storyteller.

"I hope Noah remembered to thank God," said Linda to the storyteller.

"He did," said the boy. "And he often talked to his family about God's rainbow and the love God has for each one of us."

God Calls Abram

(GENESIS 12:1–21:3)

he storyteller began a new story. "Abram was an old man about seventy-five years old. He loved God very much and spent much time talking to Him. Through Abram, God showed His people His love for them in a new way. One day the Lord said to Abram, 'Leave your home and go to another land. I will show you the way.' Abram heard God and immediately he and his wife, Sarai, put everything they owned on the back of a mule and started walking."

"How did Abram fit everything in his house on a mule?" asked Tom.

"When my family moved here," said Gail, "we came in a moving van."

"How many miles did Abram and Sarai have to go?" asked Bill.

"Did they have to walk all the way?" asked Tai, a boy who had been quiet until now.

"I'll bet Abram was scared," said Tom.

"I would have been, especially at night," said Linda.

"That's 'cause girls scare easy," asserted David.

"Sometimes grownups get scared, too," the storyteller went on, "but Abram and Sarai trusted God and went anyway."

"It must have been very hard for them to leave all their friends and relatives and their hometown," said Gail.

"They went to a land called Canaan, a land God chose," said the storyteller. "It was far and, even though they were old, they walked all the way.

"God made Canaan their very own country and promised it would belong to their family forever. Then God gave them each a new name—Sarah and Abraham.

"God also promised Abraham and Sarah a son," the storyteller went on. "God asked them to call their son Isaac, which they did, just as God asked them."

Jennifer tapped Bill on the shoulder and said, "They were obedient."

"Yes," said Bill with a sigh, "but sometimes it's hard to do exactly what someone else asks you to do."

The children all agreed with Bill.

Jacob's Ladder

(GENESIS 28:2–22)

his is a story about Jacob," began the storyteller. "Abraham's son, Isaac, was Jacob's father."

"That makes Abraham a grandfather," said Gail to Linda, who agreed.

The storyteller went on. "One day, after Abraham's grandson Jacob grew up, he decided to travel to another country."

"Did he have to walk, too?" asked Gail, who didn't like to walk.

"Yes, he did," said the storyteller. "And when he got tired, he would lie down on the grass. Sometimes he fell sound asleep."

"Sometimes I lie on our grass and go to sleep," said Tai. "One time I even had a dream." And he lay back down on the floor and closed his eyes.

Jennifer poked him. "You can't go to sleep now. You'll miss part of the story." The children laughed.

The storyteller smiled and said, "While he was sleeping, Jacob had a dream. In his dream, he had a very special meeting with God. Jacob dreamed he saw a ladder going up into heaven, with angels climbing up and down."

"I like ladders," said Tom.

"In our house we have a ladder that goes up to the attic," said Gail, "but it only has eight steps."

"I'll bet Jacob's ladder had two hundred steps," said Tom.

"I don't know how many steps there were," the storyteller went on, "but God was standing on the top step and He spoke to Jacob. He told Jacob that He was Abraham's God and Isaac's God too, and that He would give Jacob and his family the land he was sleeping on.

"God also promised to take care of Jacob, and He reassured Jacob that no harm would come to him while he was on his journey. God also promised to stay with Jacob and bring him back to this land.

"Jacob woke up very excited. He said, 'I'm going to name this place the house of God and the gate of heaven!' And Jacob called the place Bethel. The name Bethel means 'the house of God.' It became his new home."

Tom grinned and said, "I'll bet Jacob was glad he got tired and fell asleep and had that dream."

"I'm going to rename my baby brother Jacob," said Jennifer. "He's always sleeping."

Everyone laughed.

Joseph and His Brothers

(GENESIS 37:1–36)

"Joseph was a boy with many brothers," said the storyteller. "Eleven brothers, as a matter of fact. They all knew that their father, Jacob, loved Joseph best, since Joseph was born when Jacob was very old. Jacob was very happy to have God bless him in his old age with an unexpected son."

"Joseph was his father's favorite," said Gail turning to Linda.

"One day Jacob gave Joseph a beautiful coat with many colors in it. This made the brothers very angry and jealous," said the storyteller. "The brothers began to feel that Joseph was getting all the attention and they weren't getting any, so they wanted to kill Joseph. But instead, they sold Joseph to some traders for twenty silver coins. The traders took Joseph to Egypt on their camels. There they planned to sell him to somebody as a slave."

"Poor Joseph," said Linda, almost ready to cry.

"I don't like those brothers at all," said Tai, and he put his head down.

"Sometimes I get angry like those brothers when things don't go my way," admitted Bill.

"Then, do you know what Joseph's brothers did?" asked the storyteller. "They dipped Joseph's beautiful coat in animal blood and brought it back to their father.

" 'Joseph got killed by a wild animal,' they told their father, 'and nothing is left but his coat.' Jacob was so upset that he cried."

"Oh, Joseph's poor father," said Linda. "It must have broken his heart."

"But Joseph was still alive in Egypt," said the storyteller. "God takes care of everyone. Even when things go wrong, God uses the things that happen to bring us closer to Him, if we listen to

Him. The traders sold Joseph as a slave to an important family. This family took good care of him. God had a special reason for having Joseph in Egypt—so he could help his own family later on."

"If we don't stop to listen to God," said Linda, "we could miss what God wants us to do, couldn't we?"

"Yes," answered the storyteller. "God has His own way of doing things, and many times does them in ways we don't expect."

"Will you tell us more about Joseph?" asked Tom. "I'll bet some exciting things happened to him in Egypt."

Joseph in Egypt

(GENESIS 41)

he king in Egypt kept having dreams he couldn't understand, and he became very upset," continued the storyteller. "In one dream the king saw seven fat cows eaten by seven thin cows. In another dream, the king saw seven thick pieces of wheat swallowed by seven thin pieces of wheat. The king was upset by his dreams."

"Those sure are funny dreams," laughed Jennifer.

"What did the king do?" asked Tai.

"The king tried very hard to find somebody who could help him understand his dreams, and he finally sent for Joseph," answered the storyteller.

"Why?" asked Bill.

The storyteller looked at Bill and answered, "Because he had heard that Joseph could tell what a dream meant. Joseph explained to the king that sometimes God sends us messages through dreams. Then Joseph said, 'God is telling you He is sending Egypt seven good years for farming and then seven years when nothing will grow.'

Joseph also said to the king, 'A wise man will store up food for the seven bad years.' "

"Saving food is a pretty smart thing to do," Bill said to Jennifer.

"The king thought so too," responded the story-teller. "He was pleased with Joseph's words of wisdom and placed him in charge of Egypt's food supply. He made Joseph governor of all the farms and storehouses. He also gave Joseph a beautiful ring so people would know how important Joseph was. And people would bow down before Joseph."

"I knew that something good would happen to Joseph!" exclaimed David.

"Through Joseph and the king, God took care of all the people and saw that they had all the food they needed," added the storyteller.

"What happened to Joseph's father, Jacob?" asked Tai.

"Poor Jacob," said Linda. "He didn't even know that Joseph was still alive."

"He was probably still looking at the coat he gave Joseph," Gail sighed.

"I'll bet," said Tom, who was always betting, "that the story has a happy ending."

"I'll bet you're right," said the storyteller. "God blesses and loves all His people. Jacob trusted in God and showed his trust by the way he lived."

Joseph Saves His Family

(GENESIS 42–45)

hen you're hungry, what does your stomach do?" asked the storyteller.

"Mine grumbles and growls," called out Tom.

"Mine, too!" echoed the others.

"Well, that's the way old Jacob felt, because there was no food in his home. His eleven sons were hungry, too. There was no food anywhere in his country. So Jacob sent some of his sons to Egypt to buy food."

"That's where Joseph was!" exclaimed Gail with a smile.

"And he was in charge of the food," added Linda, smiling too.

"That's right," said the storyteller. "And when the brothers spoke to Joseph in Egypt, they didn't recognize him. But he recognized them as his brothers."

"What did Joseph do?" asked Bill, who was very impatient to hear what would happen. "Did Joseph tell them who he was?"

"Not right away," answered the storyteller. "First,

Joseph asked them questions about their family, which reminded them of what they had done to Joseph. And they were very sorry for what they had done."

"What happened then?" asked Bill, still impatient.

"Joseph was so glad to see them that he couldn't wait any longer. He had to tell them who he was. He said, 'I am your brother and I forgive you.'"

"I'll bet they were happy," said Tom.

"Joseph's brothers were very happy that he was alive," answered the storyteller, "and were also truly sorry for what they had done to Joseph. They finally knew how good their brother was and couldn't wait to return home and tell their father the good news about Joseph."

"Good old Jacob would like to hear the news," said Gail to Linda, and she agreed.

"Then Joseph invited his father and all his brothers to Egypt to live," said the storyteller.

"There they lived in nice houses and had plenty of food to eat."

"And then their stomachs didn't grumble or growl anymore," added Jennifer. And the rest of the group laughed with her.

"I feel good now," said Linda. "I'm happy that Jacob and his whole family got together again."

"I knew they would," added Tom.

"That's a great story," said Tai, smiling.

"I'm glad Joseph was understanding and patient with his brothers," said David.

The storyteller added, "It was good that Joseph listened to his brothers and heard their viewpoints, too, instead of being angry at them for what they had done to him. That really helped Joseph deal with his unhappy feelings."

"Sometimes listening really helps," added Bill. "I like it when somebody takes the time to listen to me."

"That's how God is, too," said the storyteller. "He loves people and wants to help them so much that He would rather wait until people work things out with one another, so they know how understanding and forgiving He is. When people keep working problems out with one another and really learn how to forgive one another, they feel happy and grow closer to one another and to God."

The Baby Moses

(EXODUS 2:1-10)

od was still helping His people to grow. He kept them together as a people, even though they didn't have their own country and had to live among the Egyptians. But the Egyptian king used God's people—the descendants of Jacob and all his sons—as slaves.

"One day the king of Egypt got angry at God's people who were living in his country and ordered his soldiers to kill all their baby boys."

Linda's eyes got big as she said, "All of them?" And she moved closer to Gail.

"Yes," answered the storyteller. "But God was watching over His people, as He always does. One mother was very afraid that she couldn't protect her child from the soldiers. So the mother saved her child, who would have been killed, by hiding him in a basket in the tall grass by the river. The baby's older sister hid nearby to see what would happen."

"Was he just a tiny baby?" asked Gail.
"I'll bet he cried a lot," said Tom.
"You would too if your mother left you alone in the tall grass," Gail answered back.

"Every day the king's daughter took a walk by the river," continued the storyteller, "and on this day she found the baby in the basket. 'Oh, look,' the princess cried, 'a baby! He's crying.' As she picked up the baby, her heart was filled with love for him and she wanted to keep him.

"Then the baby's sister came out from where she was hiding and asked the king's daughter if she wanted someone to feed the baby for her. The princess replied, 'Yes, and I will give him a name. I'll call him Moses.'"

"Why did she call him Moses?" asked Bill.

"Because Moses means 'I took him out of the water.' That's where she found him," explained the storyteller.

"I wonder who his sister got to feed him?" Linda asked out loud.

"I'll bet she ran to get Moses' real mother," guessed Tom.

"You're right," said the storyteller. "His own mother took care of the baby Moses. And nobody else knew. She thanked God for saving Moses from death. Because the princess liked the baby, she adopted him as her own son. Women are very important to God. They take care of people, just as God does."

"Moses must have been very special to God," said David.

"God guides each of us in a special way," answered the storyteller. "For example, God saved Moses so he could help save God's people and form them into a nation. Just as Moses' mother found a way to protect her child, God found a way to protect His people."

The Burning Bush

(EXODUS 3:1–7:10)

 od knew how badly Moses and His people were being treated. And now that Moses was getting bigger and older, God decided to show His love through Moses by helping His people return to their own homeland. One day, while Moses was watching his sheep, he saw a burning bush. He went up to it and was he surprised to see that the bush was on fire, but it wasn't being burned up! Then a voice from the bush called out, "Moses! Moses.'"

"I would have been surprised, too," said David, "if I saw a burning bush like that one."

"I don't like to go near fires," whispered Linda, almost to herself.

"I never heard of anything on fire that didn't burn up," added Bill, nudging Jennifer.

"Neither did I," said Jennifer.

"I'll bet God used the fire to get Moses' attention," said Tom.

"You're right again," continued the storyteller. "God sometimes uses surprises to let us know He is present to us. And the voice calling 'Moses' was the beginning of a special thing that happened between Moses and God. Then Moses answered, 'Here I am.' Next, God told Moses to take off his sandals, because he was standing on holy ground. God continued, 'I know how cruel the king is to my people. So tell the king you want to take my people out of Egypt. Go and talk to him.'

"Moses told God that he couldn't speak well. So God told Moses, 'Your brother Aaron is a good speaker. Aaron will be your spokesman. Take him to the king and I'll tell you what Aaron is to say.' That way, Aaron shared God's plan with Moses. So in spite of their own fears, Moses and Aaron went to the king, just as they had been told. They knew that God was really concerned about them and would provide whatever they needed."

"I'd be afraid to talk to a king," said Linda softly to Gail.

"Oh, talking to a king would be so exciting!" exclaimed Jennifer.

"Is a king like a president of the United States?" asked Bill.

"Something like that," answered David.

"I don't know anybody who ever talked to a president," said Gail.

But Bill was curious. He said, "I wonder what happened to Moses and Aaron."

Moses and Aaron See the King

(EXODUS 7:10–13)

 oses and Aaron went to see the king," the storyteller went on. "Aaron told the king that God wanted him to let the Israelites—God's people—leave Egypt. But the king said no, and he wouldn't listen.

"Then God whispered to Aaron to throw his shepherd's stick down in front of the king. And guess what happened. The stick turned into a snake, alive on the floor!

"In reply, the king called his wise men and told them to throw their walking canes on the floor. And each cane turned into a snake."

"All of them!" said Jennifer excitedly.

"Wow! A whole roomful of snakes," cried Bill.

"Oh, I don't like snakes," whispered Linda to Gail.

"I'll bet Moses and Aaron will win," said betting Tom.

"Don't be too sure," David answered back.

"Tell us what happened," said Gail. "I want to hear what happened."

"What did they do?" asked Linda, covering her face with her hands.

"Aaron's snake swallowed all the others," said the storyteller. "But still the king wouldn't listen to Moses and Aaron, just as God had predicted. But Moses wasn't worried. He knew God would somehow save His people and convince the king to allow God's people to leave Egypt. God told Moses that He still loved His people and asked him to be patient. The day would come when the king would willingly let the people leave Egypt. Moses knew what a stubborn man the king was and how much it would take to convince him.

"Moses and Aaron didn't always understand how God was using them to free His people. Sometimes it seemed the people were worse off than ever before, but Moses and Aaron knew that God would make everything all right in the end."

Across the Red Sea

(EXODUS 12:31–14:31)

oses and Aaron went to see the king ten times. Finally, the king said it was all right for the Lord's people to leave Egypt. So Moses led God's people toward the Red Sea. As soon as Moses and his people left town, the king changed his mind. He sent soldiers after them. When the people saw the soldiers coming, they said to one another, 'Now we're in real trouble.'

"Then God said to Moses, 'Don't worry, trust me and do what I say. Point your shepherd's stick at the sea and the water will move so you can all walk across.' So Moses pointed his stick, and a dry path appeared in the water. Then the people crossed safely to the other side.

"But the soldiers followed. They were marching across the same dry path when God told Moses, 'Point your stick at the sea again.' This time, when Moses pointed his stick, the water came back together. All the king's soldiers were caught in the middle of the sea and they drowned."

"God really protected Moses and the people, didn't He?" asked Linda, turning to Gail. Gail smiled back and nodded yes.

And Bill said, "I don't always hear God's messages to me. I wish I were more like Moses."

And Tai added quietly, "I wish I had a magic stick like his."

God Feeds His People

(EXODUS 16:1–36)

 oses led the Lord's people into the desert," said the storyteller.

"Why did they go there?" asked Bill. "There's nothing but sand in the desert, and it's very hot too!"

"Nothing grows there," said Gail.

"There's no water there either," added Linda.

"I'll bet the people got hungry and there was nothing to eat," said Tom.

The storyteller leaned forward to Tom. "That's exactly what happened. Some of the people said that Moses was a fool. Others said, 'We should have stayed in Egypt.' The people found so much to complain about that they were always grumbling.

"God knows how we feel. He wants us to get in touch with our own feelings and tell Him what we need. So Moses reminded God how hungry the people were and how they were grumbling.

"Moses showed care for his people's needs, and so did God," the storyteller continued. "God said to Moses, 'Each day I will make bread fall from the sky so the people can eat. Tell the people to pick up only as much as they need. Don't worry. The people will feel secure when they see that I take care of them each day.' The next day the people saw white flakes on the ground."

"Was it like snow?" asked Linda.

"Or frosted cereal?" wondered Gail.

"What did it taste like?" asked Bill.

"When you're in the desert, you don't have a menu," commented David. "You eat whatever you find."

"Every day for years and years, as the people wandered through the desert, the Lord fed them this way," said the storyteller. "God loves people's bodies as well as their hearts and minds. That's why he fed them this special bread. The people called this bread *manna*."

"Can people buy manna in the supermarket?" asked Tai.

"I don't think so," answered the storyteller.

"Well, I sure would like to taste it," said Bill to Jennifer.

And Jennifer nodded, saying, "Me, too."

"Loving people means sharing with them, the way God does," said Linda.

"And feeding people when they are hungry," added the storyteller, "is one way we are reminded that we need each other."

"I'm getting hungry," said Gail.

"Do you think if we prayed God would send us some manna?" asked Bill.

"He already takes care of us," answered the storyteller, "when He gives us ways to get the food, care, and love we need."

"But what if we were in the desert and starving, do you think God might send manna down?" asked Jennifer.

"He might," answered the storyteller. "God always cares about our needs."

The Commandments

(EXODUS 19:1–20:17, 31:18)

hile they were wandering through the desert, the Israelite people saw a big mountain. It was covered with white clouds. Some people heard the sound of a very loud trumpet coming from the mountain. So Moses climbed to the mountaintop. He knew something important was about to happen. And it did! He met God!

"God told Moses how He wanted His people to live. They were to love God, honor their parents, and tell the truth. They were to help each other and respect each other's needs. God wanted Moses to remember all His Ten Commandments, so God wrote them on two stone tablets. The Commandments were a gift from God to show people how to love God and how to love one another. The stone tablets would help the people remember what God had said."

"I have the Ten Commandments at home written in a book," said Linda.

"Me, too," Gail chimed in.

"I can recite the Ten Commandments," said Bill.

"Me, too," added Tom.

"It's important to live the Commandments, isn't it?" asked Jennifer.

"Yes," answered the storyteller. "They help us to love one another better and to love God better, too. So Moses took the two tablets and walked back down to the bottom of the mountain," continued the storyteller, "where the people were waiting. He had been on the mountaintop for a long time."

"I wonder what the people had been doing all this time," said David.

The Golden Calf

(EXODUS 32:19–34:35)

hen Moses came down from the mountain, he couldn't believe his eyes. He saw his people bowing down in front of a statue that was shaped like a calf. They had made it out of gold. They were praying to the golden calf as if it were God."

"They forgot about God, didn't they?" asked Tai.

"After He gave them all that manna to eat," added Bill.

"After He saved them from the Egyptian soldiers, too," said David.

"I'll bet Moses was mad at the people," suggested Tom.

"Moses got so angry he threw down the stones he was carrying," said the storyteller, "and broke them. He did that because the people had broken their promise to Moses to wait until he returned from meeting God. Moses also smashed the golden calf into little pieces to show them the great sin they had committed. Even though Moses was

very upset because the people had turned away from God, Moses told the people he was going back up the mountaintop to talk to God again. While the people were waiting for Moses to come back, they felt a deep sense of loss of God.

"This time Moses talked with God for forty days. When Moses returned, he told the people God had forgiven them and promised His guidance again. Moses received another copy of the Ten Commandments written on stone. This proved

that even though the people had forgotten God, He still loved them. God understands that we need time to work through our weaknesses. He loves us and wants to be with us and gives us many chances to be more like Him.

"But another thing happened to Moses on the mountain. He asked God for a deep knowledge of Him. He stayed so close to God for so long that his face shone bright like the sun. When Moses returned, the people could see for themselves that Moses was very special to God. In fact, Moses' face was so bright that no one could look at him without squinting."

"Like this?" asked Jennifer, closing her eyes so she could just about see.

"Oh, look at her funny face," teased the others. "Jennifer's face is all wrinkled." And the others wrinkled up their faces and squinted their eyes in the same way.

David said, "They needed sunglasses to be able to look at Moses."

"But nobody had sunglasses in those days," continued the storyteller. "Instead, Moses covered his face with a cloth so that people wouldn't be blinded by the light."

Jennifer laughed, thinking how funny it would be to see someone walking around with a cloth over his face!

The Walls of Jericho

(DEUTERONOMY 34:5-9, JOSHUA 3:16, 6:1-27)

efore God's people found their way out of the desert," said the storyteller, "Moses died."

"Who took care of the people then?" asked David.

The storyteller answered, "Even though Moses died, God looked after His people. God shows His care and concern through all people. God made Joshua their new leader. Joshua led the people from then on.

"One day they came to a city called Jericho. God wanted them to get into Jericho. This was the place God promised would be their new home. But there was a big stone wall all around the city. The wall was thick and very high. They couldn't get inside. What could the people do?"

"Couldn't they use guns?" interrupted Bill.

"Or bomb the place?" wondered David.

"They didn't have guns or bombs in those days," said Linda, who didn't like fighting.

"Why didn't they go in and talk to the people?" asked Gail.

"Maybe the people of Jericho would have let them come in," added Jennifer.

"I'll bet something fantastic happened," suggested Tom.

The storyteller winked at Tom and went on. "God helped the people get into the city. He always provides a way. God told Joshua to have the people march around the walls of Jericho once a day for six days. On the seventh day, they had to march around seven times. Then the priests were to blow loudly on their horns. Everybody else had to yell and shout. God's people kept on shouting and screaming and didn't stop."

"Loud as the crowd at a football game?" asked Bill.

"Loud as thunder?" asked Linda, her eyes opening wide.

"After the people had been shouting for a while," continued the storyteller, "do you know what happened? The walls began to shiver and shake like Jell-O. And then the stones began to crumble and fall down. Right down to the ground. Then God's people marched into the city. Everything happened just as God had promised."

Jennifer closed her eyes and imagined that the members of the Sunday School class were blowing horns and shouting around the walls of Jericho. And the walls fell down again.

When Jennifer opened her eyes, she felt good inside. She knew God could help people in very special ways. She was glad about that and thanked God for all the help He gives everyone.

Ruth and Naomi

(RUTH)

e always hear stories about men and boys," said Linda.

"Didn't women ever do anything great?" asked Jennifer.

"Sure," replied the storyteller. "Women are just as important to God as men are. Here is a very beautiful story about a wonderful woman named Ruth. She left her own home and country to stay with her husband's mother, Naomi, because everybody in Naomi's family had died."

"She must have really loved Naomi," whispered Linda to Gail.

"I'll bet she didn't want to leave home," said Tom.

"But she left anyway," said the storyteller. "Ruth said to Naomi, 'I want your people to be my people and your God to be my God.' She stayed with Naomi because she loved her and wanted to be with her. She learned to love and know God through Naomi's people. The two women settled down in Bethlehem, where Naomi felt at home."

"I remember Bethlehem," said Bill. "That's the town where Jesus was born."

Linda turned to Bill and said, "But Jesus wasn't born yet."

"I want to hear more about Ruth," urged Jennifer. "I like her. She sounds like she would be a real good friend and really stick by you when you needed her."

"Tell us about what she did," added Linda.

"In Bethlehem," the storyteller went on, "everyone could see how good and kind Ruth and Naomi were to each other. Naomi shared with Ruth what she knew about God and made Ruth feel at home among the people. Ruth cooked and kept house and even went out into the fields to gather leftover grain."

"Left over from what?" asked David.

"When farmers harvest grain in the fields," the storyteller explained, "some grain falls on the ground. Ruth picked that up, the grain the farmers left behind."

"What's so great about that?" asked Bill.

"Anybody can pick grain," added Gail.

"I'll bet something important happened to Ruth," Tom said, thinking out loud.

"It did," said the storyteller. "Ruth took care of Naomi, and God took care of Ruth. One day Ruth met Boaz, the farmer who owned the fields. Boaz was a very, very important man. He was a relative of Naomi's. When he learned about Ruth and how her husband died, Naomi reminded Boaz of a law of their people that gave him the right to marry Ruth. So he married her. When their little boy was born, they named him Obed. When Obed grew up, he had a son named Jesse. And when Jesse grew up, he had a son who became King David. David was one of God's people who had a very special job to do."

"I've heard that name before," said Bill.

"Me, too!" added David. Everyone turned to David and smiled.

"I'll bet David was a nice person," said Tai.

Jennifer smiled and said, "God really loves men and women."

Young David
(1 SAMUEL 16:1-13)

he story of King David begins with a man named Samuel," said the storyteller. "Samuel was a famous prophet in Israel. Prophets were God's special spokesmen who reminded the people that God's ways were not always their ways. Sometimes the people did not like to hear what the prophets said.

"One day God told Samuel, 'I want you to go to Bethlehem. There I want you to visit a man called Jesse. One of his sons will become king of my people. And I want you to bless the boy with oil. He will rule my people someday.' "

"Oh, Jesse was Ruth's grandson, wasn't he?" said Linda.

"Yes," said the storyteller. "So off went Samuel to Jesse's house. He examined Jesse's many sons. God told Samuel, 'None of these is the right one.' Samuel asked if Jesse had any other sons. 'Yes,' they said. 'Our youngest brother is out taking care of the sheep. His name is David.' "

Bill nudged David who was sitting next to him, and said, "His name is David."

The storyteller went on. "When David came home, God told Samuel, 'He's the one. He will be king one day.' So Samuel blessed David with holy oil. And God stayed with David from that day on. God in His own way often chooses the most unexpected people to do very special things for him—like young David, the shepherd boy."

"Did God watch over him?" asked Linda.

"How did God protect him?" wondered David.

The young storyteller nodded to both Linda and David and said, "I'll tell you a story about David that almost everyone knows."

David and Goliath

(1 SAMUEL 17:1–52)

avid's brothers were Israelite soldiers. They were fighting an army that was invading their country. Each day young David carried food to his brothers on the battlefield. One day David heard all about the enemy's giant, Goliath, who was making fun of the Israelites. Each day Goliath would shout, 'Send a man to fight me.' But all the Israelite soldiers were afraid to fight him. David said, 'Let me fight him. I have my slingshot with me.' And before anyone could stop him, he picked up five smooth stones from the ground and went out to fight the giant. David wasn't scared because God was with him.

"God asks us not to be afraid," explained the storyteller. "When we trust God as David did, we see how God really cares for us and helps us. God doesn't expect any one of us to do things alone, without Him.

"The big giant looked at little David and laughed. As Goliath came toward him, David loaded his slingshot. He hit the giant right in the

middle of the forehead. The giant fell down dead, and the rest of the enemy army ran away. David had saved his people. The Israelites won! And everyone cheered David."

Elijah Is Fed by an Angel

(1 KINGS 19:1–8)

lijah was another good man. He was one of the prophets."

"How does somebody get to be one of God's prophets?" asked Bill.

"God gives everybody a chance to be special," answered the storyteller, "and in order to be special we try to listen to God, to learn what He is asking each of us, so we can work with Him."

"But how do people know what God wants them to do?" asked Linda.

"That's hard to answer," said the storyteller, "but it helps when you trust God and are listening for His message, the way Elijah did. Many people find some time alone when they can be quiet and talk things over with God."

"What happened to Elijah?" wondered Tai.

"There was a wicked queen who wanted to hurt Elijah," the storyteller continued. "So Elijah was forced to run away."

"Sometimes the only thing we can do is run away," said Gail.

"But then he couldn't go home anymore," said

David turning to Gail. "I wouldn't like that."

"Where did Elijah go?" asked Linda.

"He walked and walked and walked, far, far away," said the storyteller. "And one day he was so tired that he fell asleep under a tree. After a while an angel came to him and told him to wake up. When Elijah opened his eyes, he saw some bread and a jar of water next to him. So he ate and drank. Then he fell asleep again. He was still very, very tired. But soon the angel woke him up again.

"Because Elijah still had a long, long way to go," continued the storyteller, "the angel told him to eat again. So Elijah ate."

"Elijah got a lot of messages from God, didn't he?" commented Linda.

"That angel told him what God wanted him to do," added Gail.

"Sometimes God's messages come to us through other people," the storyteller went on, "or in the things that we find right in front of us, like the bread and water that Elijah found beside him when he woke up. The food was so good that Elijah walked for forty days and didn't have to eat at all during those days."

Esther Saves Her People

(ESTHER)

ooking at Jennifer, who liked stories about women, the young storyteller began the story of Esther.

"A very young and beautiful woman named Esther lived with her uncle, Mordecai. They were Jews living near Persia, far away from home.

"One day the Persian king saw Esther and fell in love with her. He took her as one of his wives, and she became Queen Esther. The king, however, did not know that Esther was Jewish.

"Some time later her uncle came to see her with bad news. All the Jewish people in Persia were ordered to be killed. It was the king's order. Haman, the chief officer, had talked the king into sending out the order.

" 'Please save our people,' Mordecai begged Esther. Esther was very upset! What was she to do? How could she save her people?

"Now in those days, a wife had to wait for her husband to send for her. But Esther knew that she must act soon. So she dressed up in her most

beautiful clothes and went to see the king, her husband. Even though he had not sent for Esther, the king was so pleased to see her that he said he would grant her any wish. So Esther asked the king and Haman to have dinner with her. The king agreed.

"After dinner was over, the king once again said he would grant any wish Esther had.

"Then Esther said, 'I ask you to save my life and the lives of my people.'

"Surprised, the king wanted to know who would ever harm her.

" 'Haman has arranged for all the Jews to be killed,' said Esther, 'and I am Jewish.'

"When the king looked at Haman's face, he knew that Esther spoke the truth. Instead of killing the Jews, the king punished Haman.

"And so Esther, a very brave woman, had saved her people."

"I liked that story a lot," smiled Jennifer. "God sure uses people's talents to help others, doesn't He?"

The Three Young Men

(DANIEL 3)

 nce upon a time in the city of Babylon," the young storyteller said, beginning a new story, "a king put up a beautiful golden statue. He placed it in the center of town where people would see it. He commanded everyone to bow down in front of the statue as if it were God. All the people obeyed the king except three men. They wouldn't bow down in front of the statue because they believed that there was only one true God.

"The king got so angry with the three young men that he threw them into a burning furnace. Hot flames danced all around but never touched or burned them. God didn't let any harm come to these three loving men.

"Outside, people could hear the young men singing as they stood in the middle of the furnace. They were singing a song that told everyone how good God was and how much He loved His people. They were happy because God loved them and they expressed their joy by singing. They wanted everyone to sing to God."

"I don't like fire," said Linda.

"I'm glad kings don't throw people in furnaces anymore," murmured Gail.

"Me, too," added David.

"I'll bet everyone was surprised to hear them singing," said Tom.

"The king was so surprised," said the storyteller, looking at Tom, "that he called the young men out of the fire. When they walked out of the furnace, they looked just the same as when they went in. Not even one hair on any of them was burned. Sometimes God does marvelous things for us. And when the king saw what happened he was moved to believe in God, too. Then the king invited everyone in his country to honor God, who had protected these three young men."

FAMILY RECORD

father_____

    born_____in_____

mother_____

    born_____in_____

brothers and sisters_____

_____

father's family_____

    grandfather_____

      born_____

    grandmother_____

      born_____

mother's family_____

    grandfather_____

      born_____

    grandmother_____

      born_____

THE NEW
TESTAMENT

The New Testament

p to now," said the storyteller, "the stories we have been sharing about God's people are found in the first part of the Bible. Many people call this part the Old Testament. These stories tell us how people experienced God. Let's see how many characters you remember from the stories we told already."

So the storyteller went to the chalkboard and began to write the names that the children called out.

"I remember the women," shouted Jennifer. "Eve was the first woman."

"And don't forget Adam," interrupted Bill.

And the storyteller wrote Eve and Adam on the board.

"There were other women," continued Jennifer. "Ruth and Naomi and Esther."

"I liked Esther," added Gail.

"Me, too," agreed Linda.

"I liked David," said David quietly.

Tom had been still up to now, but when he

spoke, he had a long list of names. "Abraham, Jacob, Joseph, Moses, Aaron, and the three young men in the furnace." The storyteller couldn't write fast enough to keep up with Tom.

"Have we forgotten anyone?" he asked as he wrote the last name. "Who was the leader of God's people when the walls of Jericho came tumbling down?"

"I know," said Bill, waving his hand. "It was Joshua."

Everyone agreed.

"And who built the boat that saved the animals and God's people?" the storyteller asked.

"Noah!" chorused at least three voices.

So the storyteller wrote Joshua and Noah on the board and put the chalk down.

As he returned to his chair, he said, "Now I'll tell you some stories from the second part of the Bible, the part many people call the New Testament. Most of these stories are about Jesus and what he did for God's people. Jesus brought God to us in a way we could understand. Jesus is a visible sign of God's love. He was a lot like Noah because he saved the people.

"Jesus' story begins with a lovely young woman who was Jesus' mother."

"I'll bet her name was Mary," said Tom.

"Yes," everyone agreed.

An Angel Speaks to Mary

(LUKE 1:26–38)

he storyteller began: "A young girl named Mary lived in Nazareth. She was engaged to Joseph, a carpenter. He used to carve furniture and tools out of wood."

"Like chairs and benches and little boxes?" asked David.

"My father has a tool room in our basement," chimed in Bill proudly.

"I got a carpentry set for Christmas," said Jennifer to Bill. "I wanted one like my big brother's."

"Joseph was a very good carpenter," continued the storyteller. "And he was planning to get married to Mary. He loved her very much. One day an angel appeared to Mary. At first she was afraid of the angel."

"I'd be afraid of an angel, too," said Gail.

"I'd run away or hide my eyes," whispered Linda.

"Even though Mary was afraid at first," the storyteller went on, "she trusted God and listened to the angel."

"I'd like to see an angel, just once," said David.

"I'll bet we wouldn't know an angel if we saw one," added Tom.

"You can tell angels, because they always talk about God," said Tai. "Angels are God's messengers. And they're nice."

"I hope Mary's angel gave her a nice message," murmured Linda.

"The angel told Mary everything was all right," continued the storyteller. "The angel's message was that Mary would be the mother of a baby boy, and his name would be Jesus. The angel said God's spirit would come to her. And her son would be called God's own Son. And he would be king over a world that would last forever.

"Mary didn't quite understand everything the angel said, but she felt happy. God's messages usually give us peaceful feelings, like Mary's. She knew God was asking her to be Jesus' mother. She told the angel she would do whatever God wanted. Then the angel smiled and left."

Jesus Is Born

(LUKE 2:1-20)

 ary and Joseph had to go to Bethlehem to be counted in a census," said the storyteller. "A lot of other people were going to Bethlehem for the census too."

"I know what a census is," called out David. "That's when you count people to find out how many there are. My father told me about the census. He said we count the people in this country every ten years."

"That's right," answered the storyteller, and he went on. "When they got there, the town was crowded. There were people everywhere. All the hotel rooms were taken. Mary and Joseph finally had to sleep in a barn. And that night Mary had her baby. It was a boy. They called him Jesus."

"You're telling us the Christmas story," smiled Bill.

"Jesus' birthday story," added Jennifer.

"Birthdays are very special days," said the storyteller, "and Jesus' birthday is a special day for being happy. On the first Christmas, even the angels

111

shared their happiness."

"Will you tell us about the angels?" asked Linda, who had gotten over her fear of them.

"All right," answered the storyteller. "A few miles away, on a hill, some shepherds were watching their sheep. Suddenly an angel appeared to them.

He announced happily that a child had been born in Bethlehem, a very special baby who was Jesus, the Lord. And then lots of angels appeared and repeated the good news. They sang, 'Glory to God and peace to everybody all over the earth!' "

"What did the shepherds do then?" wondered Bill.

"I know," interrupted Jennifer. "They went to see the baby Jesus."

"The shepherds wanted to give the baby gifts," added Linda.

And the storyteller smiled. "God is always giving us gifts, and He wants us to be happy, too, and to enjoy everything He gives us. His Son, Jesus, is a very special gift, and God sent Jesus to us because we needed a Savior so we could be completely happy forever with God."

"Oh, how wonderful God is!" answered Jennifer, clapping her hands.

And the others clapped with her.

The Child Jesus in the Temple

(LUKE 2:42–52)

hen Jesus was twelve years old, families and friends from Nazareth were going back home after a big holiday in Jerusalem. Mary thought Jesus was traveling with his cousins on the way back home. But he wasn't."

"Was he lost?" Gail asked.

"I don't like being lost," murmured Linda.

"I hope his mother and father went looking for him," said Bill.

"Mary and Joseph asked all their friends if they had seen Jesus. And when nobody had seen him, they really got worried. So they turned around and went back to Jerusalem. They looked and looked for three whole days. Finally they found him. They were very glad to see him."

"Where was he?" asked Linda and Gail at the same moment.

"He was in the temple talking to the teachers," answered the storyteller. "Jesus knew answers to all their questions about God. The teachers at the

temple couldn't believe it. You should have seen
them! And Jesus was asking the teachers questions
they couldn't answer.

"Then Jesus' father and mother appeared, and you know how mothers are!" the storyteller went on. "Sometimes they ask questions that are hard to answer, too. Jesus' mother wanted to know why he had stayed in Jerusalem. Jesus answered that he was doing his Father's work. His mother and father were a little puzzled with his answer. They wondered what Jesus meant, but right then they were glad they had found Jesus.

"Then the whole family went back home to Nazareth together. And there Jesus lived with his mother and father, and grew up to be a man."

Jennifer asked the storyteller, "Was Jesus like us when he lived in Nazareth?"

"Did he ever cry?" asked Linda.

"And laugh out loud like us?" added Jennifer.

"Did he climb trees, too?" wondered David.

And Tai asked quietly, "Did he have to keep his room clean?"

Before the storyteller could answer, Tom called out, "I'll bet he did the same things we do."

And the storyteller smiled. "I'm sure he did."

Then Bill said, "Jesus would have been a good friend to grow up with. He sounds like someone I would really like to know."

The First Apostles

(MATTHEW 4:18–22, MARK 1:16–20, LUKE 5:1–11)

 esus lived in Nazareth until he was about thirty years old," said the storyteller.

"Is that old?" asked Linda.

But Bill wanted to hear more, so he asked, "What did Jesus do when he was thirty?"

"Jesus set out to tell people how much God loves us," answered the storyteller, "so he left his home. He planned to go to different towns. But he wanted others to join him. One day as he was walking near the Sea of Galilee, he saw two brothers who were fishing. He looked at them, straight into their eyes, and said, 'Follow me.'"

"What did they do?" asked Tai.

The storyteller answered, "They put down their fishing nets and went with him. Their names were Peter and Andrew.

"The three men walked along the shore a little farther. Jesus saw two other brothers sitting in a boat with their father. Their names were James and John. They were fixing their nets so they would catch more fish. Jesus walked up to the brothers

and asked them to follow him. And they did, too.
They left their father, their boat, and their jobs, just
to be with Jesus.

"By the time Jesus had finished, there were twelve men with him. Later on, people called those men Jesus' apostles."

"I'd like to meet an apostle," said Bill.

"Me, too," echoed Jennifer and Gail at the same time.

"I'll bet Jesus would call all of us if he came here today," suggested Tom.

"I'm sure he would," agreed the storyteller.

"And we'd follow him, too," added Jennifer, nodding her head up and down.

"God speaks to people through each one of us, to let us know how much He loves us," said the storyteller. "Whenever you share with anyone how much God does for you, you are like Jesus' apostles."

"Then we can all be like apostles every day," said Gail, "can't we?"

"As long as we share with other people God's love for us," added Bill.

Linda looked up and smiled. "I can do that. I can go home and tell everybody this story. And then I'll be like an apostle, won't I?"

"Yes," answered the storyteller. "Jesus always wanted others to join him in telling people how much God loves them."

A Marriage at Cana

(JOHN 2:1-11)

ary and Jesus and his apostles were invited to a wedding," said the storyteller. "They were friends of the bride and groom. After the wedding, there was a big party for everybody."

"I went to a wedding once," called out Bill. "There was lots to eat."

"My sister just got married," Jennifer said proudly. "She looked pretty in her wedding dress."

"I'm going to get married when I grow up," announced Gail.

"What did Jesus do at the wedding? Did he have fun?" wondered Bill, getting back to the story.

"All the wedding guests were having fun eating, drinking, and talking to friends," the storyteller went on. "God made us to enjoy one another and to get together with one another to have good times. Knowing and loving one another makes us more like God—and it helps us to feel good, too.

"But Mary noticed that all the wine containers were empty. The wine was gone. Mary was concerned about the new husband and wife. They would feel embarrassed if they knew there wasn't enough wine. So very quietly, Mary said to Jesus, 'There is no wine left.' And he asked, 'What can I do about it?'

"Mary knew Jesus would help somehow. She turned to the waiters and whispered, 'Do whatever Jesus asks you to do.' And sure enough, Jesus did something. He told the waiters to fill the empty jars with water and let the headwaiter taste it.

"Then the headwaiter took a sip from the water jar. He said, 'This is the best wine I have ever tasted!' Jesus had changed the water into wine. And so there was plenty of wine for the party. Jesus did many, many good things for people. God asks us to do good things too: to care for each other, to help each other when we need things, to be friendly and willing to share just the way Jesus helped out at the wedding."

Jesus Speaks to the People

(MATTHEW 5-7, LUKE 6:20-49, 11:2-4)

ne day, Jesus went up to the mountain-top," said the storyteller, "and spoke to the people sitting and standing around him."

"I'll bet it was like a storytelling hour," suggested Tom, "when a teacher sits in the middle and the class sits all around."

"Just like we're doing now," joined in Linda.

"What did Jesus say to them?" asked Bill. "Did he tell them a story?"

"Jesus explained to them how God loves every-one and how our love can be just like God's love," answered the storyteller. "Sometimes it's hard to love those who aren't always kind or nice. But God loves us no matter how mean or unkind we are. And now Jesus tells us how *we* can learn to love in the same way. He said to treat others the same way you like to be treated."

"People I know like to be treated nicely," mur-mured Gail. "I do, too."

"So do I," echoed Linda.

"But sometimes it's hard to do that," said Bill. Jennifer nudged Bill and smiled, "I know!"

"And sometimes I don't always do the nice things that I know I would like to do," added Gail.

"Jesus explained to the people that when we ask God our Father for what we need, He will help us," continued the storyteller. "Then he taught the people a prayer—a special prayer. It began: 'Our Father, who art in heaven. . . .' "

"I know that prayer," interrupted Jennifer, "my mother taught it to me."

"I didn't know that Jesus gave it to us," Linda said with surprise.

"Would you all like to say the prayer together?" asked the storyteller.

"Yes," they chorused.

"Let's hold hands while we say it," suggested David. "When we pray that way at our house, I feel very close to everyone."

So, when all the children were holding hands, they began: "Our Father, who art in heaven, hallowed be thy name. Thy kingdom come. Thy will be done on earth as it is in heaven. . . ."

(You can say the rest of the Lord's Prayer with the storyteller and the children.)

The Man Who Could Not Walk

(JOHN 5:1–15)

esus could always find kind things to do for other people," said the storyteller. "One day, near a pond, he saw a man lying on a stretcher. That man had not been able to walk for thirty-eight years. He always had to wait for people to move him. Jesus asked him if he wanted to get well. And the man answered, 'Yes, I do. I don't want to be sick any longer.' So Jesus said, 'Okay, get up and walk.' The man looked at Jesus as if Jesus were teasing him. But when he saw that Jesus meant what he said, he tried to get up. And he did. He actually stood up! The man was cured and he could walk. Do you know what the man did then?"

They all shook their heads no. "Tell us," said Jennifer.

"He picked up his own stretcher and carried it away," continued the storyteller. "God knows how much we need to have confidence in ourselves. He helps us to believe in ourselves, like the man who picked up his stretcher. Each of us has the power

to do wonderful things when we let God work through us.

"A little later in the village, Jesus met the man again. Jesus knew how grateful the man was and how much he wanted all his friends to know Jesus as he had come to know Jesus. After that, the man told everybody about what Jesus had done for him. God shows His love to others through each of us when we share with others the good things that He does for us. Do you share with others the good things Jesus does for you?" asked the storyteller.

Everyone began to answer at the same time.

The Storm on the Lake

(MATTHEW 8:23-27, MARK 4:35-40, LUKE 8:22-25)

ne evening," began the storyteller, "Jesus and his apostles got into their boat to sail to the other side of a lake. On the way over, Jesus fell asleep.

"But a storm came up. The winds howled, making all kinds of noises. The winds blew the waves higher and higher, until the water splashed into the boat. The apostles were scared. But not Jesus! He was still asleep."

"How could he sleep in a storm?" asked David.

"I'd be scared," admitted Bill.

"My daddy could sleep through a storm," added Jennifer.

Tom said, "I'll bet Jesus was tired."

"Finally," continued the storyteller, "the apostles woke Jesus up. They asked him to save them. They were afraid they would drown. When we are worried, God want us to ask for help. So Jesus stood up in the boat and told the winds to stop. Suddenly, the winds stopped blowing and the sea became calm."

"Wow!" exclaimed Bill. "I wish I could tell the wind what to do the way Jesus did."

"Then Jesus turned around," said the storyteller, "and asked the apostles why they had been afraid."

"I'll bet anybody would be afraid in a storm like that," said Tom.

"Except Jesus," added Jennifer with a smile.

"I wonder why Jesus wasn't afraid," Gail said thoughtfully.

"Because he knew that the wind and the sea could only bring physical harm," answered the storyteller. "When we have God, nothing upsets us. When we are worried and have nowhere to turn, God knows how to help us and make us strong."

Jesus Feeds the People

(MATTHEW 14:13–21, MARK 6:34–44, LUKE 9:12–17, JOHN 6:1–14)

eople were always following Jesus," said the storyteller, "and listening to his stories. The people couldn't seem to get enough of Jesus. This time there was a big crowd in a field, the biggest crowd ever. There were about five thousand people. And they listened to him all day long."

"I'll bet everybody got hungry," suggested Tom.

"Maybe they brought lunches," said Jennifer, laughing.

"But nobody knew they were going to be there all day long," said the storyteller.

"Imagine, not eating for a whole day," said Gail.

"I couldn't do it," added Bill, shaking his head.

"Wasn't there any food at all?" asked Linda and Gail together.

"One boy had five loaves of bread and two fish," answered the storyteller, "which really wasn't enough for the whole crowd. But that didn't seem to bother Jesus. He asked the people to sit down.

Then he blessed the bread and fish. He gave the bread and fish to his apostles to pass out to the people."

"Didn't they feel silly passing out so little food with so many people?" asked David.

"You can't make enough sandwiches for that many people with only five loaves of bread," added Jennifer.

"I'll bet they couldn't even feed the first row of people," said Tom.

"Jesus asked his apostles to trust him," continued the storyteller. "Jesus knew how to really trust God. He also knew what wonderful things can happen when we let God work through us. God loves each one of us and knows how to reach us with His love at every turn."

"Well, what happened?" asked Gail.

"It was just like a picnic with everyone sitting down on the grass and eating," answered the storyteller. "And the biggest surprise was that everyone got enough to eat."

"They did?" Tai couldn't believe it.

"And that wasn't all," the storyteller went on. "The apostles gathered up twelve baskets of food that were left over."

"Twelve baskets!" shouted Bill. "Wow!"

"I hope he didn't forget something to drink," said Linda. "I always drink milk when I eat."

The storyteller smiled at Linda and continued, "Jesus taught the apostles how much good God would do through them and how concerned Jesus was about people's needs. The apostles were learning from Jesus how they could do such good things, too."

The Loving Father

(LUKE 15:11-24)

hen everyone was settled again, the storyteller began another story.

"Jesus told his friends this story: One day a young man decided to leave his family and go live somewhere else. His father divided the family's money and gave his son a part of it. And off the young man went. But soon he spent all his money. And he had none left."

"Why did the boy's father give him all that money if he knew the boy would waste it?" asked Gail.

"Didn't his father know *better*?" added Linda.

"Probably he did know better," answered the storyteller, "but the father felt it was important to let his son make his own decisions. God is like that. He gives us the freedom to make our own decisions, and He doesn't try to force us to His way of thinking. God is just like the boy's father."

"What happened to the boy?" asked Jennifer.

"He didn't have enough money to buy food or

to rent a place to live, so he had to look for a job," answered the storyteller. "But times were hard and he couldn't find work. Finally, he got a job taking care of pigs. That wasn't so bad, except that the pigs got more to eat than he did. He wasn't too happy with his job, especially because he was always hungry. Every day his stomach grumbled and growled."

All the children laughed at this, because they all knew how their stomachs would grumble and growl when they were hungry.

The storyteller continued, "Then the young man remembered how well his father took care of the workers on his farm. He hoped his father would hire him as a worker. Besides, he was really sorry for the way he had treated his father. The boy knew it would be hard to face his father, but he also knew what a good man his father was. So the young man decided to return home.

"When the young man's father saw him coming down the road, he ran out to meet his son. No, he didn't fuss at him, he didn't scold him, he didn't say 'I told you not to do it.' He was just plain happy to see him. His son was home. The son said to his father, 'I really don't deserve to be your son.' But the father said, 'No! No, my son! Don't think such things. I love you and I am happy to have you back again. Now we're going to have a welcome-home party for you so we can share our joy with our family and friends.' "

Bill said, "I like that father. My own father probably would say, 'See, didn't I tell you this would happen? Why didn't you listen?' "

"I'll bet my father would be angry if I had wasted all that money," groaned Tom.

"This father was glad to see his son come home," said the storyteller. "God is like that. He always knows how happy each of us can be, and no matter what bad things we may have done, God always forgives us and forgets about those bad things. He never holds them against us if we are truly sorry."

"I like his father. He's like God. He's nice," Jennifer said.

"He liked his family to be together," said Tai, smiling.

"And have good times together," added Gail.

The Story of Zaccnaeus

(LUKE 19:1-10)

verybody began to hear about Jesus, and crowds used to get together and wait to see him whenever he came to their town. One day there were so many people around that it looked like there was going to be a parade. One small man in the crowd was named Zacchaeus. Nobody liked him because he was a tax collector, and tax collectors got richer and richer as they collected tax money from other people. So everybody was standing in Zacchaeus' way and he couldn't see anything. Zacchaeus wanted to see Jesus because he had heard what a good man Jesus was. What was Zacchaeus to do?"

Jennifer suggested, "If I were he I would climb a tree."

"That's exactly what Zacchaeus did," said the storyteller. "He climbed a tree so he could see. When Jesus passed by, he looked up at Zacchaeus in the tree and said, 'Come on down, Zacchaeus. I want to stay at your house today.' When people heard this, they got very angry. Remember, they didn't like Zacchaeus and they treated him badly because people said he got rich by cheating others. But Jesus didn't judge Zacchaeus and went to his house anyway. Usually when we love others they

love us right back. Jesus wanted Zacchaeus to know that God loves people no matter what they do. Zacchaeus was really happy; now he knew why everyone spoke of Jesus as a good man. Zacchaeus began to wonder if he could be like Jesus."

The storyteller continued, "After dinner, Zacchaeus told Jesus he realized that he had cheated people in town. Zacchaeus promised to pay back all the tax money he had taken unfairly. Zacchaeus then thanked Jesus for showing him how to be good and how to treat people. Jesus smiled and was pleased with Zacchaeus."

"Once I stole my brother's marbles," admitted Bill, "but I gave them back. Sometimes I think only of myself and forget to think about others."

The young storyteller smiled at Bill and was pleased with him.

Even Jennifer smiled at Bill, who was sitting next to her.

"My mother says that the world would be a better place if we all loved one another more," said Gail.

"I'd like that," agreed Linda.

Jesus Cures a Blind Man

(JOHN 9)

ne day Jesus saw a blind man," said the storyteller. "In those days, if there was something wrong with you, like being blind, people didn't want to have anything to do with you. But even blind people have to eat. This particular blind man begged for money along the side of the road."

"I saw a blind man begging on the street in town," said Bill. "He had a dog with him."

"My mother always gives money to people like that," added Gail.

"I don't like to see people who can't walk," said Linda sadly.

"I wonder if they have any friends?" said Tom.

"God is a friend to all people. To God, a person's being healthy or sick doesn't change His love," continued the storyteller. "God loves everyone and uses their problems in a special way to bring people closer to Him and one another. Jesus was a wonderful friend to people like the blind man."

"What did he do?" asked Jennifer.

"Jesus felt sorry for the blind man," replied the storyteller. "He knew how the people rejected him because he was blind. So he put some clay on the man's eyes and told him to go wash it off. The man went to a pool, and when he washed his face, he could see. For the first time, he could see!

"If you were the blind person who could suddenly see," the storyteller went on, "what would you like to see most of all?"

"I would like to see colors!" called out Gail. "Blue and green and red and brown!"

"I would want to see people's faces," added Linda.

"I would like to look at trees and leaves and fruit and the different shapes of things," smiled Tom.

"And I would look at the sky and clouds and mountains—all the things that are up high," said Tai.

"I like to look at bugs and worms best of all," concluded Bill.

"Eyes are really a wonderful gift," said Gail.

The storyteller nodded to Gail and said, "The man who had been blind was happy now, because he thought that all people would finally accept him as their friend."

"I hope he found some friends," said Tai.

"He found some," continued the storyteller, "but

other people thought the man had been faking, that he always could really see. But his parents said, 'Oh, no, our son was born blind. We were more surprised than anyone else when we heard he could see.'

"One day the man met Jesus again. Jesus asked him, 'Do you believe in the Son of God?' The man said, 'Who is he? Tell me, and I will believe in him.'

"Jesus looked at him, smiled, and said, 'I am he. You are looking at God's Son.' And do you know what the man did? He got down on his knees and bowed to Jesus. He recognized Jesus as the one who had cured him. And because the blind man knew God accepted and loved him, his feelings of rejection and hurt were healed."

The Raising of Lazarus

(JOHN 11:1-45)

 he storyteller began another story. "One day Jesus heard his friend Lazarus had died. He was sad when he heard the news. And he went to see Lazarus' sisters. When the sisters saw Jesus coming, they came to him with tears in their eyes. They said, 'Oh, if you had only been here, Lazarus wouldn't have died.' Jesus said, 'Let's go to the cave where Lazarus is buried.' When they got there, Jesus asked someone to roll away the stone in front of the tomb. Then he prayed. He asked God his Father in heaven to answer his prayer, to bring Lazarus back to life. Then in a loud voice, Jesus called out, 'Lazarus, come out of the tomb.' And everybody got very quiet.

"People couldn't believe their eyes! Lazarus walked out of the tomb and stood facing his friends. He was alive. He could walk and talk. He was dead and now he was alive again. Honest!"

"I'll bet Jesus was the only one who could ever do it," said Tom to David.

"But even Jesus said it was not himself but God

his Father who did the miracle," explained the storyteller.

"Jesus was always asking God to do things for all of us, especially to make us alive again to God's friendship. Being friends is very important to God. God answered Jesus' prayers for us by letting us all be His friends again through Jesus, so that we can be as close to one another and to God as Jesus is."

"That's the miracle Jesus asked of God for us, isn't it?" asked Jennifer.

"Yes," replied the storyteller. "Making us alive again to friendship with God and with one another is the miracle that happened—and keeps happening—to us."

Jesus Enters Jerusalem

(MATTHEW 21:1–11, MARK 11:1–11, LUKE 19:29–44, JOHN 12:12–18)

esus and his friends went to Jerusalem," began the storyteller, "to celebrate a big holiday. Thousands of other people were coming to Jerusalem, too. A friend brought a young donkey for Jesus to ride on. By this time, Jesus was very popular and people got very excited about seeing him. The people began to line up on both sides of the street as Jesus rode into town on the donkey.

"Many people waved at Jesus with palm branches, and some people laid palm leaves on the ground in front of him. On that day, the people even wanted Jesus to be their king. They kept shouting good things about Jesus so everybody could hear. As they walked alongside him, the people began to sing all about Jesus and the wonderful things he had done. It was like a parade. It was a happy day for everybody.

"But deep down, Jesus knew that many of these people were only his happy-time friends, and when the unhappy times of suffering came for Jesus, many of these friends would not believe in him. They were looking for a leader who would bring only good things to them, not suffering."

"I'll bet we would all stick by Jesus," said Tom.

"We sure would," agreed Jennifer.

The Last Supper

(MATTHEW 26:17–29, MARK 14:12–25, LUKE 22:7–30, JOHN 13:1–20)

he next Thursday night, Jesus and his apostles sat down to eat supper," said the storyteller. "Jesus knew this was going to be the last time they would eat together. But the apostles didn't know that. First, Jesus washed everyone's feet."

"What did he do that for?" asked Bill, puzzled.

The storyteller answered, "Jesus was showing his apostles how to be good leaders."

"I wouldn't like anyone to wash my feet," murmured Jennifer, and she tucked her feet under her.

The other children giggled. They wondered how washing somebody else's feet was teaching anybody about being a good leader.

"The apostles didn't want Jesus to wash their feet either," continued the storyteller, "and at first they didn't understand what Jesus was doing. Some said no. Others tried to pull their feet away. But Jesus said this was important to him, and unless they let him wash their feet, they could have no

155

part of him. When Jesus said that, they immediately told him it was okay.

"Then, during supper, Jesus took some bread and passed it around so everyone could take a piece. Then he told them something else they couldn't really understand. He said, 'Eat this. It is

my body.' He did the same thing with a cup of wine, saying, 'Drink this. It is my blood.'

"This was the very first Holy Communion," explained the storyteller. "Then Jesus told the apostles they would be able to share Holy Communion with one another after he had gone away.

When you love someone and you have to go away, you like to leave them something to remember you by."

"We remember him in the bread and wine," said Bill.

"Whenever we have Holy Communion, it reminds us of Jesus," said Tai.

"In Communion, Jesus left himself to be with us," added Gail.

"Did Jesus leave anything else?" asked David.

"Yes, the Holy Spirit," the storyteller replied. "After supper, Jesus told them to love one another the way he loved them. Also, he said soon he was going back to his Father. The apostles were not happy to hear this. They didn't want him to go away. But Jesus explained to them that unless he went away they wouldn't be able to be with him forever. Then Jesus promised that they wouldn't be alone, that the Holy Spirit would come to live with them and teach them everything they needed to know. Then the apostles felt better, because they knew someone would be with them."

"I feel better, too," whispered Linda to Gail.

Jesus Is Put to Death

(MATTHEW 26:57–27:60, MARK 14:53–15:47, LUKE 22:54–23:53, JOHN 18:12–19:42)

en in power felt threatened by Jesus and were not very happy with him," said the storyteller. "In fact, they hated him."

"Why?" asked Bill.

The storyteller answered. "They hated Jesus because they really didn't understand him. Besides, they didn't want to change their way of life, which was what Jesus was telling everybody to do. They refused to believe Jesus when he said he was the Son of God. Jesus also did good things for people, which made him more popular than the men in power, and they didn't like that. So on the night before the Passover holiday, they arrested Jesus and took him to court. When Jesus came before the judges during the night, they asked him if he really was the Son of God. Jesus remained quiet and wouldn't deny it. Then the judges got very upset with Jesus."

"They weren't very kind to him," sighed Linda.

"I think they were very cruel," added Gail.

"What did they do to Jesus?" asked Tai.

"Before the day was over," said the storyteller, "soldiers beat Jesus with whips and put a crown of thorns on his head. The next day, Jesus was taken to a hill called Golgotha, where soldiers nailed him to a wooden cross. Even on the cross, Jesus prayed and asked his Father to give the men who hurt him the gift of forgiveness."

"Where were Jesus' friends?" asked Gail, puzzled. She couldn't imagine leaving a friend alone.

"Didn't anybody help him?" asked Bill.

"Didn't anybody come?" wondered Linda.

And Tom said, "I'll bet they were afraid."

"The whole time Jesus hung on the cross," the storyteller went on, "his mother, some women, and the apostle John stood nearby. They were the only ones who stayed, even though they were afraid. One of the women was Mary Magdalen. She loved Jesus and his mother. She was a good friend and knew now to be faithful, because Jesus helped her when she needed someone. She was a great woman.

"When Jesus died, some of his friends took his body down from the cross. Mary Magdalen helped wrap Jesus' body in a white sheet. Then they buried him in a cave and rolled a big, big stone in front of the opening."

"What a sad story," said Jennifer.

And David added, "It's so sad when people don't understand one another."

And everyone agreed.

"Jesus died on a Friday," continued the storyteller, "and that day is called Good Friday."

"Why is it called 'Good'?" asked Gail.

"We call it Good Friday because it was the day God showed how good He really is. Without a Good Friday there could be no Easter Sunday. We needed Good Friday so we could be friends with God again. God let His Son, Jesus, die so that all of us could pass through death with him and be able to live forever as friends."

"Why does God want us to die?" asked Bill.

"God didn't want it that way at all," answered the storyteller, "but because of sin we needed some new way back to God. So God gave us a new life in Jesus, an Easter life."

"What's an Easter life?" asked Tai.

"That's the next part of the story," answered the storyteller.

The First Easter

(MATTHEW 28:1–10, MARK 16:1–11, LUKE 24:1–12, JOHN 20:1–18)

 wo days after Jesus died, early on Sunday morning when it was still dark, Mary Magdalen and some women walked to the tomb to visit Jesus' body. But when they got there, the big stone had been rolled away. They looked inside the tomb. It was empty! Jesus wasn't there!

"The women ran back to tell Peter and the other apostles, but Mary Magdalen stayed at the tomb crying. She thought that someone had stolen Jesus' body.

"Then she noticed what looked like two men in white robes inside the cave. They asked her, 'Why are you crying?'

" 'Someone has taken Jesus away,' she sobbed.

"Then she turned around, still crying. And there stood a man. Mary Magdalen thought he was a gardener. He asked her, 'Why are you crying? Who are you looking for?'

"Again Mary Magdalen explained that her friend
Jesus had died and now his body was gone.

"This time the man said, 'Mary.'

"As soon as he said her name, she recognized

that he was Jesus. And at once she knew that Jesus was alive. He was talking to her. Now her tears became happy tears."

"Sometimes I cry when I'm very happy," said Gail.

"I would have been happy, too," agreed Linda.

"I'll bet Jesus was happy to be alive again," said Tom.

"I'll bet he was, too," answered the storyteller. "Then Jesus asked Mary Magdalen to go and tell the other apostles that she had seen him and talked with him. And she went right away to tell them."

"I think Mary must have been happy to be chosen to tell the apostles," said Jennifer.

"I'll bet they were glad to hear the good news, too," added Bill.

"Yes," said the storyteller. "That Sunday was a very, very happy Sunday for Jesus and his friends. It was the first Easter Sunday. Jesus had kept his promise and had come back from the dead, and he would never die anymore. And he told them not to be afraid of death because he would be with them when they had to die, and he would take them to a new life!"

"Will Jesus be with me, too, when I die?" asked Linda.

"Yes," replied the storyteller. "He is with all people who believe in him when they die."

The Apostles See the Risen Jesus

(LUKE 24:36–43, JOHN 20:19–31)

ne night the apostles were sitting together in a room," continued the storyteller. "The doors were closed. Suddenly Jesus was there in the room with them. He talked with the apostles and he showed them his hands. They could see where the nails had made holes in Jesus' hands when the soldiers hung him on the cross.

"Thomas, one of the apostles, was not there that night. And when the other apostles told Thomas about Jesus coming to see them, he said he didn't believe it. Thomas even said, 'I'll believe Jesus has risen only when I can see for myself and when I can put my fingers into his wounds.'

"The next time Jesus appeared to them in their room, Thomas was there. Jesus walked over to him and said, 'Go ahead, Thomas. Put your fingers into my wounds.' All Thomas could say was, 'My Lord and my God.' Jesus really understood Thomas, and now Thomas knew for himself that Jesus was really alive. It was all right for Thomas

to doubt. Jesus wouldn't reject him for that.

"Jesus also said he was pleased with those people who hadn't seen him themselves but would believe from other witnesses that he had risen from the dead."

"Like us?" asked Linda. "We have never seen Jesus and we believe in him."

"That's right," answered the storyteller. "Jesus was talking about people like us."

"That's why we need someone to tell us the story of Jesus," said David, "so we can believe that Jesus came back from being dead."

"And we all have stories to tell about Jesus in our own lives," added the storyteller. "We can all be witnesses for Jesus."

"I'll bet it's hard for some people to tell others about Jesus," said Tom.

"I think it's easy and fun," smiled Gail.

"In a way, we're all apostles, aren't we," said Jennifer, "when we tell others about Jesus."

The storyteller smiled.

The Ascension

(MARK 16:19–20, LUKE 24:44–53, ACTS 1:1–12)

 esus stayed around for forty more days. He spent much time with the apostles. They talked a lot together, because Jesus wanted the apostles to understand everything. Jesus wanted everybody to hear from his apostles what he had taught them. Soon it was time for Jesus to return to his Father.

"First Jesus asked the apostles to wait in Jerusalem for the Holy Spirit. Jesus assured them that the Spirit would come and teach them everything they needed to know.

"As Jesus was walking with the apostles to a high hill, they began to realize that he was going away, and they grew sad—they felt they would be left all alone, without their friend Jesus, because they still didn't understand all his words."

"I would have cried if I had been there," said Gail.

"Me, too," added Linda. "I wouldn't want Jesus ever to go away."

"Jesus would have liked to stay, too," said the storyteller, "but he knew it was time for his apostles to do their own work."

"Sometimes it's better for people to go away from us," said Tai. "Then we learn to do things for ourselves."

"So Jesus spoke to the apostles for the last time," continued the storyteller. "He blessed them. And slowly he began to disappear. In a few moments no one could see Jesus anymore.

"The apostles were still staring at the spot where Jesus had stood when they saw two men in white robes. The two men told the apostles that Jesus had gone to heaven but he would return again. And, until Jesus returns, they were to do the things Jesus had asked them to do."

"Who are those men in white robes?" asked Bill. "Why are they always appearing?"

"I'll bet they're angels," suggested Tom.

"I'll bet you're right," said the storyteller. And he continued, "Then all the apostles went to Jerusalem to wait for the Holy Spirit. They were beginning to learn to trust that Jesus' promise would come true. And it did."

The Coming of the Holy Spirit

(ACTS 1:13–2:47)

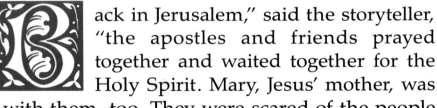 ack in Jerusalem," said the storyteller, "the apostles and friends prayed together and waited together for the Holy Spirit. Mary, Jesus' mother, was with them, too. They were scared of the people who put Jesus to death, and they locked themselves inside their house. They were afraid the same thing would happen to them now that Jesus was gone.

"One day they all began to hear a funny noise. It sounded like a big windstorm. And then suddenly tongues of fire appeared over everyone's head."

"That sounds scary," said Bill. "Whoever heard of a tongue of fire?"

"That is just a way of telling us that the Holy Spirit had come to them," explained the storyteller. "When the wind stopped and the fire disappeared, do you know what happened? They weren't afraid anymore. In fact, they were happy and excited. They all went outside and began to tell everybody all about Jesus and about the things that had happened to them."

"Is that what happens when the Holy Spirit comes?" asked Tai.

"I think I'd like to have tongues of fire over my head," said Jennifer. "I'd like the Holy Spirit to help me talk about Jesus to my friends and to everybody else."

"I'll bet the apostles told everybody about Jesus and how he came back from being dead," said Tom.

"That day there were lots of visitors from other countries in Jerusalem," continued the storyteller. "These visitors spoke only their own languages. But when the apostles began to speak, even though there was no one language everyone knew, the Holy Spirit made it possible for all the visitors to understand what was said in their own languages.

"The apostles were telling everybody that Jesus was God's Son. Then a wonderful thing happened. Lots of people came to believe in Jesus that day because of what the apostles said. And they became followers of Jesus. The apostles had started their work of going everywhere and telling everybody about Jesus."

"That's what we've been doing here," said David. "We've been hearing stories about Jesus."

"We'd be just like the apostles, too, if we began to tell others about Jesus," added Jennifer, a big grin on her face. She liked that idea. And so did the others.

Going Home

he storyteller looked up at the big clock on the wall. "It's time to go home," he said to the children around him.

"Are we finished already?" asked Gail, surprised.

"So soon?" echoed Linda.

"Wow, the time sure went fast," added Bill.

"I really enjoyed being with you today," the storyteller told them. Then he smiled and said he had to return home to his father. And to his mother.

"I wonder if my mother is here yet," said Tai. He got up and walked to the windows that looked out on the street.

Others got up and followed Tai.

Through the windows the children could see their mothers and fathers sitting in cars, waiting for them to come outside. The children all began waving their hands.

"As soon as I get in the car, I'm going to tell my parents my favorite Bible story," said Gail to Linda.

"I am, too," added Linda.

"This really was a special Sunday School class," said Bill to David.

"Yes, it sure was," agreed David.

"I like the storyteller," said Gail.

"Me, too," added Linda. "He really knew Jesus, and showed us how to know him."

"And how to love one another, too," said Tai.

They all agreed.

As the children turned from the windows, they saw the storyteller walking toward the door.

Then Tai realized that the storyteller never told them his name. "I wonder what his name is," he said to the others.

"We never asked him," answered Jennifer.

"I wonder where he lives," said David.

Just at that moment, as if he had forgotten to say something important to them, the storyteller turned around.

Before the storyteller could say one word, Jennifer, Gail, and Bill ran over to him and began talking to him, all at once.

"Do you have to leave?" asked Gail.

"Don't go," begged Jennifer.

"Will you come back?" asked Bill.

Tom, standing near Tai, whispered, "I'll bet he will."

The storyteller smiled and, touching Bill on the shoulder, looked around at all of them and said, "You will see me again."

The children smiled at him. "Okay," they said.

Then, just to make sure, Jennifer asked the storyteller, "Do you promise?"

The storyteller replied, "I will be with you always."

And with that he left as quietly as he had come. The children knew, however, that the storyteller would return and always look after them, as He was Jesus Christ, their Savior.